# FUN REA

# Down Rope Walk
# CRASH!

# Sydney Higgins

Sydney Higgins

All illustrations by George Craig

Cover design: John Grain

ISBN-10: 148198473X
ISBN-13: 978-1481984737

# TWO

# FUN READ

## STORIES

# DOWN
# ROPE WALK

by

## SYDNEY HIGGINS

A few years ago,

Rope Walk was always busy.

Then, most of the men

worked in the docks

but, even when they were at work,

there were lots of women about,

shopping and talking

while their kids

played in the street.

But now the docks were closed

and the large lorries

no longer used the street

as a short cut

to and from the docks.

Now most of the people

still living in Rope Walk

were very old.

Some of them

didn't want to leave the house

where they had spent

so much of their lives.

Others stayed there

because they were very poor

and couldn't move anywhere else.
Almost all of them
spent most of their time
behind their locked doors.

They lived in fear
of the gangs of kids
that played in the empty houses
during the day
and the tramps and rats
that hid in them at night.

Tom Keeler's gran
was one of the old people
who didn't move far
from their homes.
Tom had lived with her
since his parents split up
five years ago.

Ron Green lived next door

with his mum

but she had an evening job

and Ron didn't see much of her.

So Tom and Ron spent

a lot of time together.

They not only lived in the same street,

they went to the same school

and were in the same class.

They walked to school together

and, almost every night,

they went about together.

Yet in some ways, the two boys

were not at all the same.

Tom was short and fat:

Ron was tall and slim.

Ron loved playing football:

Tom hated playing the game.

But the two boys

did get on well together.

In the five years

they had been friends,

they had shared many good times

and together they had been

in some very tights spots.

The worst of all of these

was about to begin

when they set off

from Ron's house

late one Sunday

on a very cold January morning.

They walked slowly

up the street

through the deep snow

that had fallen during the night.

There was nobody else in the street.

'Look!' Tom said,

pointing to the doorway

of one of the empty houses.

'What's up?' Ron asked.

'Somebody's been in there,'

Tom said, still pointing.

'Look at the footsteps

outside in the snow.'

'Don't get so worked up!'

Tom said, as he walked on.

'Some tramp's been in there.'

'No!' Tom said firmly.

'More than one person

has been in an out of there.'

'OK,' Ron replied.

'So there were two tramps.

Come on, will you?

If we stand about here

we'll die of cold.'

'Let's have a look inside, Ron.'

'What for?' Ron asked.

'The tramps have gone now.'

'If they *were* tramps!'
Tom replied.

'And why shouldn't they be?'

'Because that house

was boarded up yesterday

and now – look!' Tom said,

walking up to the doorway.

'The planks of wood

that were over the door

have been pulled out.

If you give a good pull,

they'd all come down.

The street is full of empty houses

that aren't boarded up.

So why should a tramp bother

to break into this place

and then try to board it up again?'

'Because this place isn't as dirty

as all the others,' Ron said.

'Perhaps he was a clean tramp!'

Tom didn't say anything.

He pulled the planks of wood

and, one by one, they fell

into the snow at his feet.

Then he pushed the door open.

'Come on,' he said.

'Let's have a look around.'


'OK, OK,' Ron replied.

'I'll go in there first,

just in case there's a tramp inside

who's so hungry

he'll bite your head off.'


Inside the house,

there was a damp, wet smell

and it was very, very dark.

The two walked around

the two rooms downstairs

but they were both empty.

Then they went upstairs

and opened the door

into the back bedroom.

Even though it was very dark,

both of them saw

the room was almost full

of piles and piles of boxes.


'What do you think is in them?'

Tom asked, peering into the darkness.


Ron had already opened a box.

'Booze!' he replied.

'Hundreds of bottles of whisky!'


'What are they doing here?' Tom asked.


'How should I know?

But whoever put them here

was up to no good.

I mean, they must be stolen stuff.

I mean, it's obvious, isn't it?

Somebody came in here

in the middle of the night

and hid up all this booze.

That means whoever it was

is going to be back here

to pick them and

take them away.'

'So let's get out of here,' Tom said.

'Not yet!' Ron replied.

'Well what are we going to do?'

'Help ourselves.'

'We can't do that.
You can count me out!'

'Don't be daft!' Ron said.
'Whoever put them here
must have stolen them.
So they don't belong to them.
That means they won't care
if we walk off with a few bottles.
Come on, Tom!
Let's see how many of them
we can carry out of here.'

Ron had just piled six bottles

into Tom's open arms

when the door banged to.

In the pitch darkness,

they both turned round

to hear a key

being turned in the lock.

For a few seconds,

the two boys stood still

and said nothing.

It was Tom who spoke first.

'What are we going to do?'

he asked very quietly,

holding on to Ron's arm.

'Kick the door down,'

Ron replied.

'We can't do that,' Tom said.

'Somebody locked the door

and so for sure

he's still out there.

There might even be

two of them outside,

just waiting for us to come out.

'I don't think so.

If there were two or three,

they'd have come in here

and sorted us out.

I bet there's just one of them

and he was left here

to keep watch.'

'But we don't know that.

We're in a trap!'

'No, we're not!' Ron said.

'There's this window.'

'But it's boarded up!'

'It won't be in a bit,

when I've smashed it.'

Ron unlatched the window

and pushed it up.

Then, after a few pushes

and smashes with his fist,

he broke off the boards

that had covered the window.

Light and cold air

flooded into the room.

Ron pushed his head

out of the open window

and took a quick look

at the back of the house.

Below was a yard

with a high wall all around it.

He saw there was no point

in trying to climb down

because he wouldn't be able

to escape from there.

'The only thing we can do,'
Ron said, 'is to climb up
onto the roof.'

'I can't get up there,'
Tom said, backing away
from the open window.

Ron looked at his fat friend
and said, 'Perhaps not!
Still, not to worry!
I'll climb up there
and bring back some help.
It won't take long.
You won't come to any harm.
Is that OK?'

'Sure,' Tom said.
'You go and get back here

as fast as you can.

I don't want to be here on my own

if some gang's coming back here.'

'Keep cool, mate.' Ron said.

'I won't be long.'

Ron climbed onto the windowsill.

Close by was a drainpipe.

He took hold of it and pulled.

It would hold him.

'See you soon, Tom,' he said.

Ron grabbed the pipe with both hands.

Tom couldn't bear to watch.

He moved away from the window

and sat down on some of the boxes.

Slowly, Ron moved up the pipe

until he reached the gutter

where he managed to pull himself

onto the snow-covered roof

He pushed his body
deep into the soft white snow.

With his feet on the gutter,
he held tight onto roof tiles
and then began to edge slowly
along the roof.

Every move he made

sent showers of snow

falling into the yard below.

He was very, very cold.

His hands seemed to be freezing.

What he was hoping to do

was to move along the roof

until he found a house

where someone lived.

Then he would be safe

because he knew everybody

that lived it the street.

After he'd edged past

a couple of houses,

he stopped.

Above him was a chimney.

Fixed to it, there was

a television aerial.

He felt sure that this house

was the one where Miss Yates

lived with her old mother.

The only problem was

how he could get off the roof

and climb down into the back yard.

He knew he had to move quickly

if he was going to help Tom

who was locked in the bedroom.

The robbers could well return

at any minute.

As his left hand groped

through the wet snow,

he touched something strange.

He pulled on it and saw

that it was a brown cable.

He pushed away the snow.

He made sure that both his feet

were secure in the gutter

and his right hand was firmly

holding one of the roof tiles.

Then he pulled hard on the cable.

Snow flew up

but the cable held fast

to the chimney.

Gripping the cable tightly,

he used his left foot

to clear the snow out of the gutter.

Soon he found

what he was looking for –

a hole in the gutter.

This meant that, beneath it,

there would be a drainpipe

he would be able to use

to climb down into the back yard

of Miss Green's house.

He wasn't afraid.

He just knew that

there was no time to waste.

Slowly, slowly,

holding tight to the brown cable,

he slid carefully down the roof

until his left knee was resting in the gutter.

He pressed down to be sure

it would not break

under his weight.

Slowly, slowly,

still holding tight to the cable,

he moved down his right leg

and managed to slip his foot

between the drainpipe and the wall.

Then, holding the cable in one hand

and the gutter in his other,

he lowered his left leg

further down the drainpipe.

Slowly and carefully

and still gripping the cable,

he lowered himself.

At first, he held the guttering

but then he moved both his hands

to the drainpipe

and held on tightly.

After that, it was easy

for someone as fit as Ron

to climb down the drainpipe.

Still frozen but very pleased

with himself,

Ron quickly reached the backyard.

Then a door opened

and an angry woman came out,

waving a frying pan above her head.

'What you doing?' she shouted.

'Miss Yates! It's me! Ron!'

She peered at him for a moment

and then lowered the frying pan.

'What on earth are you doing

climbing all over my roof

and down my drainpipe?' she said.

'You could have broken your neck

or frozen to death!'

'Sorry if I scared you, Miss Yates.'

'Sorry? I should think you are.

I heard all those noises.

I thought you must be a robber!'

'Well that's it, Miss Yates.'

'What's it?'

'Just up the road,' Ron said,

'there are some robbers.

They locked up me and Tom.'

'Tom? Is that Tom Keller? I know his mum.'

'Yes. But he's still locked up.

I managed to escape.'

'You better come in then,'

Miss Yates said,

taking Ron by the arm.

'You look frozen to death.'

As soon as they were inside the house,

Ron tried to brush the snow

off his wet clothes.

'It's very cold out there,' he said.

'Take off your wet coat.

I'll make you a nice warm drink.'

'No thanks,' Ron replied.

'It's very kind of you

but I must get going

to see what's happened to Tom.'

'Well, what has happened?'

'We went into Mrs Nelson's old house

and, while we were upstairs,

somebody locked us in a bedroom.

I got out but Tom's still there.'

I have to go.'

He opened the front door

and was about to leave

when he saw that a car and a lorry

were parked outside the house

where Tom was trapped.

There were also two men

standing in the street.

Ron quickly went back inside.

'I can't go out there.

I bet they're looking for me.

Do you have a phone,

Miss Yates?' he asked.

'A telephone?' she said

and Ron nodded his head.

'Of course we don't.

Why would we want a telephone?'

'But I must do something!

I need to phone the police.'

'I'll show you what you can do,'

Miss Yates said and led Ron

into the front room.

'Here,' she said.

'Put this coat on.'

'But it's a woman's coat!' Ron said.

'I know.' she replied.

'You just put it on.

If those men out there

are looking for you,

they won't stop a woman.

The coat's a bit big for you

but it will do very well.'

Ron put on the coat.

Then he rolled up

both legs of his trousers,

took off his shoes

and put on some old slippers.

Miss Yates then tied a scarf

round his head.

'There,' she said.

'I bet your mum wouldn't

know it was you.'

'Thanks, Miss Yates,' Ron said.

'I must get going now,

God only knows what those men

may have done to Tom.'

He then ran out of the room.

'Stop!' Miss Yates shouted.

'You have to go

a bit slower that that

or nobody will think

you're an old woman.'

'Thanks, Miss Yates,' Ron said.

'You're right. I forgot.'

Ron was almost at the front door

when a very old woman

came down the stairs.

'Here!' she called.

'What are you doing?'

What are you doing with my coat?

You've stolen it!' she shouted

and tried to hit him.

'Sorry!' Ron said.

'I've got to go.'

The old woman stepped back.

'It's a man,' she said.

'It's man in my coat!

'It's all right, mum,'

Miss Yates said to her.

'It's Ron from up the road.

You know, Mrs Green's son.

I've lent him the coat.'

'But it's my best coat,'

the old woman said.

'No, its not, mother!

It's your old coat

and he'll bring it back.'

'Thanks!' Ron said,

as he opened the front door.

'Off you go,' Miss Yates said.

'And let me know how things went.'

'And bring my coat back!'

her mother called.

In the street, Ron saw

the two men walking

up and down in the snow.

Ron walked past them

with his head bowed down.

They took no notice of him.

Outside the house

where he'd left Tom,

there were another two men

loading boxes into the lorry.


When he got to the end of Rope Walk,

Ron started to run through the snow

towards the phone box

outside the old dock gates.

His trousers rolled down

as he ran along

and his headscarf

fell off into the snow.


When he reached the phone box,

he rang the police

and told them about the house

and the boxes of whisky

and how he escaped

and how Tom was still there.

Then he ran back to Rope Walk.


He arrived before the police.

A man was closing up the lorry.

and two others were getting

into the car.

Ron started to run down the street

but he slipped and fell.

Before he could get up,

two police cars came up the street

and skidded to a stop by the lorry.

Four policemen jumped out

and shouted at the men,

telling them to get out

and stand against the wall.

Four of them did

but one ran up the road towards Ron.

Ron stood up and, as the man ran by,

he stuck out his foot.

The man fell over it

and landed with his face

flat in the snow.

A policeman ran up

and grabbed hold of the man.

'Thanks, young man,' he said to Ron.


'Man!' said the thief

who had been running away.

'I thought it was some old bird!'


'Come on!' the policeman said.

'In the place where you're going,

you won't be seeing any birds –

old or young.'

He marched him off

to join the other four men.

Ron walked after them.

'Are you the lad who phoned?'

one of the policemen asked.

'Yes. It was me,' Ron said.
'But where's my mate, Tom?
They locked him in that house.'

'What have you done with the lad
that was in the house?'
a policeman asked one of the men.

'There was nobody there,' he replied.
'I think he climbed out
through a window.'

'He must be in there!' Ron said
and ran into the house.
'Tom! Tom!' he called
as he ran up the stairs.
'Where are you?'

The door of the front bedroom opened
and Tom called, 'I'm here!'

'How on earth did you get in there?'
Ron asked. 'I left you
in the back bedroom.'

'I know,' Tom replied.
'But when those thieves came in,
I hid behind the boxes.

They saw the open window

and said that's how

we must have escaped.

When they started

moving out the boxes,

they left the door open.

So I nipped out

and hid in the other room.'


As Ron and Tom were talking,

a policeman came upstairs.

He thanked both boys.

Then he wrote down their names

and where they lived.

'When we've locked up

this gang of thieves,

we'll be back in touch

to take your statements.'

Left alone in the house,

the boys walked into

the empty back bedroom

where they had found

all the boxes of whisky.

'It's just not fair,' Ron said.

'We went through all that

and didn't even manage to drink

even one drop of whisky!

# CRASH!

by

# SYDNEY HIGGINS

# I

'I wish I were you,'
Paul said to Nick.

'What on earth for?'
Nick asked.
He could not see
why anybody should want
to change places with him.

'You've got it all,'
Paul replied.
'Your dad's got lots of cash.
You live in a big new house.
All the girls fancy you
and the boys think you're great.

You're good at games

and you're clever as well.

Then to cap it all,

your dad buys you

anything you want.'


'Sorry,' Nick said.

'I wish I hadn't told you

my dad had got me a car.

I just didn't think

you'd get upset.'

'I'm not upset,' Paul snapped.

'All right,' Nick replied.

'So you're not upset.

Look! I'll tell you what.

Why don't you come over

on Saturday?

Then you can have a drive

in my old car.'

'Can I?' Paul said.

'Can I really?'

'Of course you can,' Nick said.

'Come around after lunch,

say at about three,

and we'll drive the car

round and round the field

for an hour or so.

Then you can have tea.

How about it?'

Paul smiled happily.

'Can I really?' he asked.

'Of course you can,' Nick replied.

'But you need to know

it's just an old, old car.

My dad didn't buy it.

He was given it because

it's not safe to be on the roads.'

'Are you sure it'll be OK

with your folks?' Paul asked.

'Sure they won't mind?'

'No they won't.

They won't be at home

on Saturday afternoon,'

Nick said.

'There's some garden party

in the village

and mum and dad

will have to go.

My dad's opening it

and so he's got to be there

to make a speech.'

'Great!' Paul said.

'I'll be there at three.'

'Shall I ask my dad

to come and pick you up?'

'No need,' Paul said.

'I'll come on my bike.'

'Will you be able to find

our house?' Nick asked.

'Nobody can miss it.' Paul replied.

'It's the biggest house

in the village.'

Nick let this go

and said nothing.

It wasn't his fault

that he lived in a big house

and his dad was well off.

In any case, there were

two other boys in their class

whose dads had given them

old cars to drive around in.

The field at the back of their house

wasn't being used.

So why shouldn't he drive around it

in his car?

After all it was an old car

that had cost nothing.

If his dad hadn't brought it home,

it would have been

just a load of scrap.

He liked having his own car,

even if Paul didn't seem

too happy about it.

Any boy of fifteen

would want to have his own car

even if it was full of rust.

## II

Paul lived in a busy town

about five miles away

from the pretty village

where Nick lived.

Just after two o'clock

on Saturday,

Paul set off from his home.

After a while, he had left behind

the crowded streets of the town.

He liked cycling

along the empty country lanes.

It was so much quieter

than the town where he lived.

It was a warm day.

The sun was shining

and the birds were singing.

Paul was very happy

as he biked towards Nick's house.

He had never been asked

to go there before.

But he knew where it was

because he had passed it

several times

while out on his bike rides.

Paul would have liked to live

in a big house like Nick's.

His house was much smaller

and his dad didn't earn

anywhere near as much

as Nick's dad did.

His dad had scraped and saved

so he could send Paul

to the posh private school

that Nick attended.

Paul liked it there

but there were times

when he hated being

one of the poorest boys there.


Paul arrived at Nick's house

just before three.

He stopped at the end

of the long gravel drive

and stared at the large, pink house.

There were huge trees

on both sides of the drive

and, in front of the house,

was a large pond.

Floating on the pond

was a home-made raft.

Paul knew that Nick used this

when he fished for carp in the pond.

He had seen all this before

when he cycled past the house,

praying that Nick wouldn't see him.

But, this time, he'd been invited there

so he could drive Nick's car.

Nick came out of the front door

to welcome Paul.

'Great to see you!' he said.

'Glad you could make it.

Just stick your bike

over there in the garage.

Then we'll go round the back

and you can see the car.'

The bike was quickly parked

and the two boys hurried round

to the back of the house.

They ran through the garden

and into the field.

'Well what do you think of it?'

Nick asked.

'It's great!' Paul said.

Then he banged the roof.

'Don't hit it too hard,'

Nick said and smiled.

'It might fall to bits!'

Then he asked Paul,

'Have you ever driven a car?'

'Not really.' Paul replied,

'but I'm quick to learn.'

'That's great,' Nick said.

'I'll take her for a spin first

and tell you what to do.

Then you can have a go.

Is that OK?'

'Sounds good to me.'

'Right! Jump in

and with luck it'll start

and then off we'll go.'

The two boys got into the car.

Nick turned the key

and the engine roared.

Then he put the car

into first gear and there was

a  loud grating noise.

'Sorry about that,' Nick said.

'The clutch has almost gone.

So it always makes a din

when you put it into gear.'

Then off they went,

driving in a large circle

round the field.

Because the car had been driven

along that track many times,

there was no grass there

and so clouds of dust were thrown up

behind the car.

The rest of the field

was covered in long grass.

Because of this and the dust,

Paul could see very little

but the well-worn track ahead.


'It goes a fair old speed,'

Paul said, holding on to his seat

as Nick swung the car

round the dust track.


'Yes,' Nick replied.

'It's not a bad old car

but it seems as though

we're going faster than we really are.'

Nick stopped the car.

'Fancy having a go now?'

he asked Paul.

'Yes, please,' Paul replied.

'OK. I'll get out,' Nick said,

'and you can move across.'

The two boys changed places and

Paul got ready for his first drive.

'There's not much to it,'

Nick told his friend.

'There are three pedals

down there on the floor.

The one on the left

is the clutch.

The brake is in the middle

and on the right

is the accelerator.

Your left foot works the clutch

every time you change gear.

You use your right foot to press

either the brake or the accelerator.

You have to take care

that you don't press down

the accelerator by mistake

when you want to stop!'

Nick continued.

'Now the gears are simple.

Just think of an H.

First gear is straight up and

second gear is straight down.

Third gear is to the right

and then straight up.

Fourth is then straight down

from third. Got it?'

Paul nodded.


'Anyway,' Nick said.

'don't worry about it.

You'll soon get the hang of it

but, to start with, you need

only the first and second gears.

You need to take it easy

at first till you get used to it.

Now there's just one more thing.

I said the clutch has almost gone.

This means you have to put

your left foot down hard

when you change gear,'


Nick looked at Paul and said,

'Right! Now start her up

and have a go!'

Paul turned the key and

pushed his right foot down

on the accelerator.

The engine roared.

Paul thought for a moment

and gripped the steering wheel.

Then he pressed down the clutch

and pushed the gear lever

upwards, trying to find first gear.

There was a loud grating noise.

'Don't worry about that.'

Nick said. 'It is in gear.

Let your foot of the clutch

slowly and you're away.'

Paul did as he had been told

and the car jerked forward.

Then the engine stalled.

'Bad luck!

You forgot to accelerate,'

Nick said. 'You've got

to let the clutch up

and then your right foot has

to ease down on the accelerator.

Have another go.'

Paul started the engine again.

This time all went well

and the car moved off.

'That's it,' Nick said.

'Now change into second gear

and get up a bit more speed.'

As Paul drove along,

Nick gave him some tips

on how to drive:

'Feel for the gear stick.

Don't look down …

Don't pull the steering wheel

round too quickly …

Don't brake as you corner …'

Paul did as he was told.

The car sped along the track

and the dust flew up behind.

'This is great!' Paul said.

'It's just like a race track!'

He was very happy.

'Thanks,' he said, turning to smile at Nick.

'Watch out!' Nick shouted.

Paul looked and saw that the car

was heading off the track.

He pulled the steering wheel hard

but the car veered sharply

to the other side of the track

and on into the long grass.

'Brake!' Nick called

and Paul slammed his foot down.

He missed the brake

and hit the accelerator.

Nick pulled on the handbrake

and switched off the engine

but this did not stop the car.

With a crash and a thud,

the car slammed hard

into the deep ditch

at the side of the field.

The two boys lurched forwards.

Paul hit his head

on the steering wheel

and both of them

banged their knees

against the dash board.

For a moment, they didn't say

or do anything.

Then they both started to laugh.

'That was close,' Nick said.

'Are you all right?'

'I think so,' Paul said.

'It's just my head

but I think it's OK.

I just hit a bump.

It wasn't my fault.

There was a big bump.'

'It's all right.' Nick said,

'But let's get out

and see what the damage is.'

The ditch was deep

but it was also quite narrow

and so only the front of the car

had gone into it.

Nick jumped down into the ditch

and peered at the front of the car.

'Oh my God!' he exclaimed.

'What's wrong?' Paul asked

as he too jumped into the ditch.

Nick had no need

to say anything.

Paul saw for himself

that the left wing of the car

was badly smashed.

'But I just hit a bump,' Paul whined.

Nick ignored him and said,

'It's only the wing.

I'll just pull it off.

The car will go without it.

Let's hope the engine's OK!'

'Shall we start it again

and see?' Paul asked.


'No,' Nicky replied.

'Not until we've got the car

out of the ditch

and I can have a look to see

if anything else has been smashed.'


The two boys got out of the ditch

and stared at the car.

The back wheels were off the ground.

The front bumper was pushed

deep into the earth

on the far side of the ditch.

It wasn't going to be easy

to get the car out but

they decided to try.

They got hold of the back bumper

and tried to pull the car out

but it would not move.

'Oh, God!' Nick said.

'I hope dad's in a good mood

when he gets back.'

'You're not going to tell him,

are you?' Paul asked.

'Of course I am,' Nick replied.

'But I only hit a bump,'
Paul said again. 'I didn't mean
to put the car in the ditch.'

'Don't worry about it,' Nick said.
'We'll get a tractor to pull it out.'

'I think I'd better go,' Paul said.
'I hate rows. It wasn't my fault!
I'll pay for the damage. Honest!'

Nick could see Paul was upset.
'I'll tell you what,' he said.
'Let's get out of here.
We'll go to the garden party.'

# III

Mr Watson, Nick's dad,

did not stay long at the garden party.

His wife stayed there

because she was giving out

the prizes later in the day.

Walking along the road

that led to his house,

Mr Watson met Nick and his friend.

They didn't have much to say

perhaps, he thought, because

there was a fairground there

and lots of pretty girls.

Mr Watson didn't mind.

He was feeling quite merry.

There had been a beer tent there

and he'd had quite a lot to drink.

Mr Watson went upstairs

to change his clothes.

He stood at his bedroom window

and looked out at the back garden.

He turned away and then

quickly turned back again.

He had seen the crashed car!

As he stared at it in the ditch,

he became very angry –

not because it had been crashed

but because Nick had not said

anything about it.

Mr Watson could not work out

why his son had said nothing

but he intended to find out.

He put his jacket back on

and set off again

to the garden party.


When he got there,

he looked around for Nick

and saw him on a rifle range.

As there were lots of people about,

he did not want to talk to Nick there.

So he walked up to his son and said,

'You come back home with me.'

Nick said nothing.

He knew that his dad

had found out about the car.

The two walked home in silence.

When they arrived at the house,

Mr Watson went straight to the field.

Pointing at the car, he said,

'Well, Nick. What about that?'

Nick told him about the crash

but his dad was still angry.

'I don't care about the car,'

he said. 'But I do care

that you said nothing about it

when we met just down the road.

Why didn't you tell me?

When were you going to say

something about it? Never?'

Because his dad kept on

firing questions at him,

Nick was unable to say anything.

'Give the boy a chance to speak,'

a voice said. It was Mrs Watson

who had just got back home.

Mr Watson was now very angry.

'All right,' he said to his wife.

'You can deal with him.

I wash my hands of the car.

I'll have nothing more to do with it.'

And he didn't.

Mrs Watson got a tractor

to pull the car out of the ditch.

Then Nick quickly found out

it was so badly damaged

that it would never go again.

On Monday at school, Nick told Paul

that the car was all right.

But he never invited Paul

to visit his house again.


And the car?

It's still in the field.

Nick keeps his pet rabbits in it.

Printed in Great Britain
by Amazon